To Deli!
Thank You to

MW00935265

Josh's Book

Joshua Wesolek

READ IT 4 HER

joshsbook.com

ISBN-13: 9781731252173

DEDICATION

To Jennifer,
Thank you for loving me through all the messes.
Thank you for giving me a reason to try.
Thank you for saying, "yes."
I Love You.

CONTENTS

ACKNOWLEDGMENTS

I'd first like to thank my Lord and Savior, Jesus Christ, for showing me what real love is. I'd also like to thank my wife, Jenni, for letting me practice my relationship skills on her over the years. Next, I'd like to thank my parents, Mike & Carol, for training me up in the way I should go. Finally, a special thanks to all my friends, family, and co-workers who have trusted me enough over the years to share their relationship struggles with me. We learn a lot when we ask for help.

PREFACE

Hey guys. My name is Josh. Before I tell you about myself or what you're about to read, let me first say how much I RESPECT you for even opening this book! I know how hard it can be for us guys to ask for help, especially when it deals with mushy stuff like feelings. It's even harder when we don't know what's wrong – or worse yet – when we don't think ANYTHING'S wrong. So, just the fact that you picked this book up, opened it, and are actually reading this, proves that you have the courage to at least acknowledge that things could be better in your relationship. And I'm here to help – or at least try my best.

So, who am I? Well, let's start with who I'm not. I'm not a doctor or psychologist or therapist or anything like that. I don't have any degrees in Female Brain-ology or claim to know everything about relationships. Actually, who I am is a foundry guy and a husband who's been with my wife for 26 years. In that time, I've seen, heard, and made a lot of mistakes and did my best to learn from them. I'm also a chaplain who has had the opportunity to hear from and offer counsel to many couples over the years who have trusted me enough to share their relationship struggles with me. For that, I am truly humbled. Also, because I am a Chaplain, even though this isn't a "religious" book, you're likely to see a few

Bible-y words here and there. I just can't help it, but I think we'll be ok. So, that's me. Now, what about the book?

Well, basically, what you're about to read is a collection of tips and insights that I've put together based on my experiences as a boyfriend, fiancé, husband, and chaplain over the years. Pointers for things that we as men typically struggle with in a relationship (whether you realize it or not). Just bits of advice that I wish I had known at the beginning of my relationship. Some of these lessons are pretty simple. Others were hard to learn. In fact, I'm still working through some of them today. That's why I wrote this book. I want to help you avoid having to learn this stuff the hard way.

Now, I realize that this book isn't going to apply to every relationship or cover every issue you might be facing; but if even one topic can help strengthen the relationship between you and your girl, that's what matters. We guys have to stick together and have each other's backs! It's rough out there in Relationship Land, and I truly hope, with the help of this book, that you and your girl will live happily ever after in it.
(Oh, and don't be surprised if she reads it too.)

Thanks.

You got this.

JOSH'S BOOK

JOSHUA WESOLEK

I

SAY, "I LOVE YOU"

Let's start this out with an easy one. Go tell your girl, "I love you." Sounds simple, right? Well, think about it. When's the last time you actually said the words, "I love you" to her? And I'm not just talking about a half-hearted, mumbled, "love you" as you're walking out the door to go to work. I mean, a stop what you're doing, look her in the eyes, "I LOVE YOU." Was it today? Yesterday? Do you remember the last time you actually said it? And, no, texts don't count. Kinda' fuzzy? I know. It's easy to just go through day to day life with the understanding that you love each other. You might even be thinking, "She knows I love her. Just look at everything I do for her." And, yeah, that's probably true. But there's a little corner tucked away in every girl's mind that holds onto random doubts and "what ifs" - however irrational - and she needs to be reassured from time to time. Just letting her ASSUME you love her isn't enough. She needs verbal confirmation. You need to say it. Yes, she sees what you do for her, and she appreciates it and loves you for it, but in this case, actions don't always speak louder than words. She knows you love her, but at the same time, you haven't said it in a while, so do you really? (Yes, your girl actually thinks like that sometimes. No, it doesn't make sense.) Remember, there's a big difference between saying you love her and showing you love her. Both are important and necessary, but there's just something about verbal confirmation that's comforting and reassuring for her. That being said, there's also a HUGE difference between a passing, "love you" and a sincere, direct, "I love you." The "I" makes it personal. It affirms your connection to her and erases any doubts. Guys, she needs to hear you say the words. She needs to KNOW that you love her.

So, tell her. Often.

2

NEVER STOP WINNING HER

While speaking about relationships, my dad will say, "Keep her by the same means you won her." I love that. Come to think of it, that could be the theme of this entire book. Once you've won your girl's heart, it's not time to congratulate yourself, put her up on the mantle, and stop playing the game. The game has just begun, my friend. If you don't defend your title – you could lose it. (That means you could lose her, if you got lost in my gaming metaphor). By the way, I'm in no way implying that your girl is simply a trophy or an award to be won, but she is incredibly valuable, and you should do all you can to keep her. Think back on all the effort you put into courting her. I'm guessing there were lots of long, late night conversations, letters, gifts, little affectionate touches and glances, and flirty winks and giggles. All those things you did to "make her like you" eventually paid off when you won her over and she rewarded you with her exclusivity. You did all the right things and won her heart, but the thing is, you should NEVER STOP winning it. You see how beautiful and valuable she is. That's why you tried so hard to win her over in the first place; and now that you have, you need to keep showing her that you still see her that way. Don't bait and switch! Now that you're together, keep having the long talks. Keep buying her little gifts "just because." Give her a little flirty touch as you pass by her in the hallway. Yes, even the winks and giggles should stay. Keep treating her as though you're still trying to win her heart. Yes, you may have already won it, but when she sees how much value you've placed on it, and the effort you continue to put into keeping it, you'll never stop winning her over.

3

LISTEN TO HER

I don't know how many times my wife will "remind" me of something when I'm POSITIVE that it was the first time I was hearing about it. I put "remind" in quotes, because I KNOW that she's NEVER mentioned this thing before. Whether it be a lunch date she's going on, or when I have to pick up the kids, or whatever. I don't remember EVER being told this thing! Now, ninety-nine percent of the time, yes, she has told me before – don't tell her I said that! The problem is, that we as guys have a focus issue. We focus on one thing at a time. If we're watching a show, that's all we're doing. If we're working on something in the garage, that's it. All our focus tends to be on the task at hand (even if that "task" is playing golf on our phone). Girls, on the other hand, have minds like supercomputers. They can process a billion bits of information simultaneously! They can be cooking dinner, typing an email, talking on the phone, getting the kids' clothes out for school, and watching a TV show all at the same time. So, in the midst of all that, when the thing she needs to tell us comes to mind, she will tell us, fully expecting us to be able to process that one bit of information despite our being fascinated by a pizza commercial at the time. The reality is, we hear her when she says things. We might even respond with an, "uh huh" - but we're not really listening. Our focus isn't on her, so, whatever she just said doesn't stick because it just got pushed out of our head by something MORE IMPORTANT. Wait. What? Yeah. When you constantly forget what she says, when you forget appointments, and when you keep forgetting she asked you to do something, she can start to feel like she's not important enough for you to listen to. She may also start to feel that she has to compete with the things that you DO pay attention to. That's a slippery slope guys. Don't make her compete for your attention. Show her that she's your priority. Pause the movie. Stop cranking the socket wrench. Look at her when she's talking. Acknowledge her. Focus on her. Listen to her. She's what's important.

4

BE A GENTLEMAN

It's sad to say, but it seems that real gentlemen are a dying breed these days. I was watching an old show from the 40s or 50s and a guy was taking his girlfriend out on a date to the local soda shop. Just a casual time of dessert and conversation. Only there was nothing "casual" about it – at least by today's standards. He was dressed in a shirt, tie, and jacket and she had on a nice dress. He opened every door for her, pulled out her chair and treated her like she was the most important person on Earth. ALL his attention was on her. Now, I know this was just a TV show, but it was representative of the culture of that era. My, how far we've moved away from that. Not everyone, of course, but it seems that what once was commonplace has become such a rarity. You, no doubt, have noticed that sometimes when you hold a door open for a woman walking into a store, she may respond with a big smile or a, "that was nice of you." You may have also heard, "Wow! Apparently, chivalry isn't dead!" The fact that they react that way shows you that gentlemanly behaviors are not that common anymore. Speaking of chivalry, do you even know what that means? I sorta did, but I had to look it up, and what I found was pretty cool.

CHIVALRY /'SHivəlrē/ *noun: The combination of qualities expected of an ideal knight, especially courage, honor, courtesy, justice, and a readiness to help the weak.*

Wow! Doesn't that sound like a gentleman? Doesn't that sound like the kind of man you want to be? Doesn't that sound like the kind of man your girl would like you to be? I especially thought the knight reference was fitting because girls are always looking for their "knight in shining armor." Are you hers? And I'm not just talking about on special occasions. It's easy to open doors and pull out chairs when we're out to a formal anniversary dinner or some snazzy black-tie event. But what about every other day? She's just as important then, isn't she? If you don't already, start trying to incorporate some chivalry into everyday life. Carry the groceries in from the car for her. Let her fix her plate first at dinnertime. When you go for a walk, make sure she's on the side away from traffic. When you go on a date, put all your focus on her and NOT on your phone. And yes, open doors and pull out chairs. Whether you're at McDonald's or a Michelin Star restaurant, be her knight in shining armor. Be uncommon.

Be a gentleman.

5

PAY ATTENTION

If she were to ask you, right now, to run to the store and get her favorite candy – would you know what to get? What's her favorite color? Her favorite flower? Favorite smell? The last time you went walking around the mall together, did anything catch her eye? What's her taste in clothes? Ok, that was a lot of questions, but knowing this stuff is very important. I'll give you a few reasons why. The first (and I think, most important) reason is that when you know the answers to these types of questions, she'll feel valued and know that she's important enough to you that you want to know all about her. Another reason is that gift giving becomes much more personal and meaningful when you get her specific things that you KNOW she likes. For example, while talking about our kids and books they like, my wife mentioned that her favorite book when she was little was a Dr. Seuss book called *McElligot's Pool*. She said she read it so much the cover fell off. That could've just been some random trivia lost to the dustbin of history – but I was paying attention. A quick online search later, and I bought a copy of the book to give to her on our anniversary. She loved it.

Not because it cost a lot, but because it MEANT a lot to her that I was paying attention to her. One more reason that knowing about her is important, is that by actively watching and listening for clues and insights into her likes and dislikes, it keeps you from becoming a passive bystander in your relationship. Don't just be a placeholder. If you don't know the answers to the questions above, find out. Be engaged. Be present. She's a very unique and intricate person. Trust me, she's worth learning about.

Pay attention.

6

BUY HER ICE CREAM

Ah, ice cream. *Insert dream sequence here* I'm pretty sure if guys suddenly ceased to exist, ice cream would be the next logical relationship choice for girls. There's just something awe-inspiring about the connection between a pint of chocolate chip swirl and the girl who's emotionally eating the whole thing. Ice cream is there for her when she's happy, when she's sad, when she's tired, and when she's mad. That is, of course, until it isn't. Because she didn't buy any. How sad. I couldn't tell you how many times I've seen girls pass up something they wanted because they "don't need it." Or because they feel like that money could be better spent on something for their guy or their kid or a bill or whatever. And I'm not just talking about ice cream. It could be anything they enjoy: a favorite snack, a manicure, a new dress, a night out with her friends – anything. Sadly, girls can sometimes fall into a habit of prioritizing other people or situations higher than themselves and their own needs and wants. Why? Well, I won't pretend to know every reason, but there are two major ones that I've noticed. The first one is that girls tend to be natural caregivers. They need to make sure that the people around them are ok. Whether that's you or their kids or their parents or friends, they are wired to make sure that they're taken care of. To accomplish that – as is typically the case with any caregiver – they tend to ignore their own needs. This is why she won't buy that cute purse she saw because she knows that your work boots are getting a little worn and she wants to make sure you stay comfortable and safe on the job. The second reason girls will deny themselves things they enjoy is body image. Girls are often their own worst critics when it comes to how they look. We could be drooling right in front of her, and she would still be self-conscious about her hips or arms or belly, etc. This is why she avoids going shopping for herself or going out with her friends or, yes, buying that delicious pint of ice cream. Does she want to do these things? Of course, she does. Can she rationalize them all away with a ton of excuses? ABSOLUTELY! And she's really good at it. What YOU need to do is see past the excuses to what she's really saying. You need to help her treat herself. She does SO much for everyone else, she deserves to be rewarded. She deserves to do the things that make her happy. Help her make that happen. Tell her your work boots are just fine. Let her know how beautiful she is in that new outfit she's trying on. When you ask her if she wants you to bring home some ice cream and she says, "No. . I don't need it." BUY IT ANYWAYS! (I mean, obviously, if she's legitimately dieting and trying hard to get fit, don't sabotage her. But in general, buy it!) She takes care of everyone else; make sure she takes care of herself, too. Encourage her to do the things that make her happy. The next time she tries to talk herself out of something you know she wants, it's your turn to be the caregiver. Put her first.

Help make her happiness happen.

7

MAKE EYES AT HER

I'm gonna' go out on a limb here and assume that you probably think your girl is cute. Well, of course you do. There's a good chance that she thinks you're cute, too. It's only natural. That's a pretty big part of being attracted to someone! But guys and girls process attractiveness very differently. Guys are very visual, whereas girls tend to be more emotional. Ask a guy what attracted him to his girl and you'll likely hear answers like, "she has a nice smile" or "I love her eyes." But when you ask a girl, you'll probably hear things like, "he listens to me" or "he makes me laugh." Girls just tend to respond more to feeling than they do to visual stimuli. But, just for now, let's focus on looks. If you ask either a guy or a girl if they think their significant other is cute, of course they're gonna' say, "yes." That's easy. But try this. If you put a guy in front of a mirror and ask him if he thinks that he, himself, is attractive, you'll probably get a little chuckle followed by something like, "yeah, I'm not too bad – hey ladies. . ." Now try that with a girl and you'll have a whole different story. Girls will laser focus on some area that makes them feel less attractive. They might say things like,

"this shirt makes me feel fat" or "I don't like my legs."   Meanwhile, we're peeking around the corner like, "Heeeyyy!"   And that is EXACTLY what you need to be doing. You need to help her FEEL attractive. How? By letting her know how you see her.   Whenever she comes around, whether she's dressed to impress or in an old pair of sweats and a faded t-shirt with paint on it, MAKE EYES AT HER. And make it obvious. Move your eyebrows up and down. Give her elevator eyes. Heck, whistle if you have to. Just let her know that even if she doesn't believe she's a hottie when she looks in the mirror – you do.   Even if you have to exaggerate the eyebrows and throw in a, "how YOU doin'?"; and even if you get an eye roll and a, "no" in return, just keep doing it. Remember, she's emotional, and even if it's hard for her to accept how attractive you think she is, she WILL know how attractive you make her FEEL. Body image is a big deal for girls. They don't always like what they see in the mirror, so, instead, let your eyes be her mirror. Whenever she looks into them, let them reflect how beautiful you know she is. I bet before too long, she'll start to see what you see.
And seeing is believing.

8

LET HER CRY

Most girls cry. A lot. They cry while reading a touching post on social media. They cry when they're tired. They cry when they're happy. They cry when a particularly emotional car commercial plays on the TV. You get the idea. At some point, she's gonna' cry. And what's our first response? "What's wrong?" We're instantly in MUST FIND REASON AND STOP CRYING mode, right? And that's nice of you, but hold on a second. God designed girls with a treasure trove of emotions and an extraordinary capacity to store them up. And store them they do! A customer was nasty with her three days ago. That's in storage. Her kid just freaked out at her about homework. In storage. Something she saw just reminded her of a hard time in her past. Storage. Well, eventually, all this stored up emotion needs to come out. Most of the time it comes out as tears. Psychologists even call these "emotional tears;" and they've been proven to rid the body of stress hormones and release endorphins. It's a way for her to FINALLY stop for a moment. To purge the system. To release the pressure of everyday. A chance for her to let go of all the dirty looks, disappointments, frustrations, and anxieties that have been building up for who knows how long. The bottom line is, she NEEDS to cry. It's how she's designed. It's not surprising for my wife to say, "I don't know" when I ask why she's crying. It took a long time to learn, but when I hear that now, I let her know I'm available, give her a kiss on the forehead, and leave her be. Just let her cry. She'll let you know if she needs you.

9

DON'T FIX IT

Ugh...this one is hard for me. After twenty-six years together, my wife still has to call me out on this. I am a fixer. I think most guys are – or at least we try to be. When we are presented with a problem, our instinct is to formulate a solution and correct the issue as soon as possible. Whether that problem is a burned-out lightbulb, a leaky faucet, or a squeaky hinge, IT WILL BE FIXED! Now, for projects around the house or with the car or at work, being a fixer is an admirable and invited trait. However, when it comes to your girl's feelings and emotions, you're gonna' have to take off the tool belt, I'm afraid. Anytime my wife is in a bad mood or sad or upset, obviously, I ask her what's wrong. (GUY STEP #1: IDENTIFY PROBLEM SO I CAN FIX IT!) As soon as she tells me, I immediately pull out the verbal duct tape and get to work telling her the solution to her problem. (GUY STEP #2: FORMULATE A SOLUTION SO I CAN FIX IT!) But then, unbelievably, instead of praising me for my amazing wisdom and insight, and thanking me for finding the solution that had been eluding her for so long, she says, "I don't need you to fix it!" Woah! Wait a minute! What

about (GUY STEP #3: FIX IT!)? This is what I do!
Why would she NOT want me to fix it? Well,
first of all, she's not dumb. Chances are, she
already knows the solution to the problem and
your unsolicited suggestion could actually feel
demeaning to her. She's not looking for a fix.
She's looking for emotional support. Her
feelings are hurt and you can help stabilize her
by just being there. By being understanding,
validating her feelings, and listening to her. If
she's truly looking for a fix, she'll ask for your
help. But, until then, put the duct tape away!
Try giving her a long hug instead.

10

PROVIDE FOR HER

The Bible says that if a man isn't willing to work, he doesn't eat. This verse has been misconstrued and taken out of context for years. Quite recently in the political arena, as a matter of fact. But I don't want to get into theology and politics. Basically, the principle here is, if you are able to work – you should. As men, we're typically thought of as the providers for the household. (Again, let's not get all P.C. here). We work to pay the bills, buy stuff for the house, buy stuff for our girl, put food on the table, and if you have kids, make sure they have everything they need. Ok, yes, we do it to buy stuff for ourselves, too, from time to time. And that's great. Working is necessary to generate income and maintain a certain standard of living. But some guys take this working thing to the extreme. They think that providing for their family means they need to make as much money as humanly possible. If a man won't work, he doesn't eat. But these guys want to eat steak and lobster every night. They're not happy with a 12-gig data plan on their phones. They need to have unlimited! Twenty channels on the TV? No way! They need the ultra-deluxe package with 390 channels, DVR, and unlimited streaming movies! Now that's providing! But, in order to pay for all this "providing", he works seven days a week. Overtime? Yes! Holidays? Yes! Birthdays? Anniversaries? Yes! Yes! It's very difficult for these guys to turn down any opportunity to make money because that is what providing means to them. Unfortunately, while they're working all these hours, their families are missing out on one of the most important things that a man should be providing for them – his time. Being present. Some guys get their priorities mixed up and the acquisition of wealth becomes number one. They think that a ton of money in the bank and getting their girl a new car or the latest cell phone or buying her the latest fashions is showing his love and dedication. Are you one of those guys? Do you think the amount of money you make represents how much you love your girl? Let me ask you this. What good is that beautiful dress, if you never see her wear it? What good is the latest cell phone when the only interaction she gets from you is a text or rushed call to say you're working over? What good is that steak dinner when she's eating it alone? Sure, those things are nice, but she didn't get into a relationship with stuff. She got into a relationship with YOU. That means you need to be part of it. I bet if you asked her, she would gladly drive a used car, talk on last year's cell phone model, wear an outfit from Target, and eat fast food, as long as it meant she could do all those things with you. Yes, we need to provide, but there are a lot of other things to provide than just things. She needs your time. She needs your touch. She needs you to listen. She needs your emotional connection. She needs you. Not your money. Take a good look at your priorities. Find a balance. Take an unexpected day off from work to spend with your girl. Show her that she's your priority. Because, even though you won't be making money spending time with her, you'll still be providing her with the one thing she needs the most. You.

II

GO ON DATES

This one is going to focus more on married or long-time couples rather than those still in the courting phase. Those in newer relationships are often said to be "dating", so let's assume that these couples are actually doing just that. I want to direct this topic to those couples who have been together for years. Those who are living together, maybe with kids, have jobs and meetings and hobbies. The ones who think they need more hours in the day while they juggle grocery shopping, taking the kids to cross country practice, hair appointments, and all the other seemingly never-ending life stuff. Is that you? Then you need this. I want you to do something. Stop reading this for a minute and think about a typical day in the life of you and your girl. Actually, think about a whole week. Go ahead, take your time. I'll wait. . .

Done? Great. Now what did you see? Did you see days that run one into the other? Are they cookie cutter duplicates? Did you see your job, shopping, mowing the lawn, watching TV, running out of toilet paper, and going to bed too late? Sure you did. Most of the time, all we see is the day to day routine that plays out over and over again – the things we have to do. But tell me something. When you were thinking through your day to day activities, do you remember seeing that time you and your girl went out for dinner at a favorite restaurant - just the two of you? Or how about the time you took her to the movies and walked around the mall holding hands? Wait. You mean you don't remember those parts? Trust me, you're not alone. Life sneaks up on us. We're creatures of habit. We set our alarms for the same time. We like to go shopping on certain days over others. We cut our grass on the same day. Well, eventually, these habits became routines and those routines became a daily itinerary of how our lives need to be run. But often times, that itinerary gets so full that it doesn't leave room for any deviation. And, in this case, by deviation I mean going on dates! Don't let life make you forget that the girl you're living with is the same girl you bent over backward trying to impress years ago. The same girl you excitedly picked up to go out for ice cream. The same girl you MADE THE TIME FOR no matter what. Make the time again. Deviate from the itinerary. Yes, she's your partner and together you make your household work. But somewhere inside, she's also still your girlfriend. Show her you remember that. Show her that spending quality time with her is a priority. Show her that you're still excited to be "dating" her; that she's the one who makes this crazy life worthwhile. *Don't let routine suffocate relationship.* Break away from the day to day and take her out on a date.

I'm betting your girlfriend will be right where you left her.

12

LOOK AT HER

What color are her eyes? Does she have freckles? Did you ever notice that scar before? Does her nose crinkle up when she smiles? When is the last time you REALLY looked at your girl? I'm not talking about the passive look to see where she's going when she gets up off the couch. I'm also not talking about any sort of sexualized looking that guys are known for. (Yes, she saw you look, by the way.) I'm talking about a long, purposeful look that sees the smallest details. The kind of look when you're snuggled up together watching a movie and suddenly realize that she's so much more captivating than ANYTHING on the screen; or lying in bed while she sleeps and remembering how ridiculously lucky you are to wake up next to such an angel. The kind of look that notices the permanent swirl in her hair you never noticed before or the little cluster of freckles on her shoulder. Maybe while you're holding her hand you notice that she broke a nail and the polish is chipping off and you're reminded of how hard she works every day. Look close enough and you can see the tiny teeth marks in her forearm from when the baby mistook her for a teething ring. Look deep into her eyes, and you could get lost for a while.

Unfortunately, some guys are afraid that if they look too closely, they might find some imperfections. Well, let me save you the suspense – you will. NONE OF US are perfect specimens. But that's sort of the point. You want to know the little secrets. The hidden birthmark. The tooth that pokes out just a little farther than the rest. The toes that curve in a little. It's these little peccadillos, these little details that only you know about her that make her uniquely yours. A testament to the closeness and intimacy you share. It's part of the whole package that makes up the perfection of her. So, if you haven't in a while, TAKE SOME TIME and look at her again. REALLY look at her. That's the girl you fell in love with, remember?

Take another look.

JOSHUA WESOLEK

13

SEE HER

You've no doubt heard of the Tooth Fairy. If you lose a tooth, you place it under your pillow at bedtime and when you wake up, there's money where the tooth was! You didn't see anything. Didn't hear anything. But the money's there, so, the tooth fairy must have come! Amazing! The Tooth Fairy does all the work behind the scenes and you reap the benefit! Well, in my house, I'm extra lucky because there are tons of fairies! The Laundry Fairy. The Dishes Fairy. The Shopping Fairy. In fact, my wife and I comment about them fairly often. For example, I'll take the last bottle of water from the fridge on the way to work, and when I get home, they're completely restocked! I'll tell my wife, "Hey! The Water Fairy came!" Another example is, if I reach into my top drawer and I'm all out of socks, I'll tell my wife who responds with, "Well, I guess the Sock Fairy hasn't come yet!" Come to think of it, when she talks about the fairies, it always sounds a little sarcastic. Hmm. Anyway, these fairies do EVERYTHING! I go to work and come home and stuff is clean, folded, vacuumed, etc. Sometimes it even happens overnight – just like the Tooth Fairy! I'll wake up and, BOOM, the cupboards are restocked! It's awesome!

Ok, ok, I think by now, you're picking up what I'm putting down. There really aren't any fairies. But there is an AMAZING wife who miraculously keeps the house running and clean and stocked. She always keeps the kids in the right sized clothes. She helps with homework. She does so, so much – but, working second shift, I don't often see her doing it. It happens when I'm at work or sleeping in or whatever. But even though I don't see it, I still reap the benefits of it. Yet, how often do I ACKNOWLEDGE her efforts? How often do I let her know that I SEE HER and how amazing she is? Probably not enough. What about you? Do you have a fairy in your house? Is your girl always working behind the scenes so that all you see are the benefits? That can be a very lonely place for her. A woefully under-appreciated place. So, the next time you climb into bed and notice that the "Linen Fairy" put fresh, clean sheets on it, pull her close and let her know you appreciate her. You're amazed by her. You're so THANKFUL for her. Let her know, even though you may not actually see her do all she does, that everywhere you look – you SEE her.

JOSHUA WESOLEK

14

GIVE HER SOME QUIET TIME

I read somewhere that a woman's mind is like an internet browser. There are 74 tabs open, six of them are frozen, three pop-up ads are blinking, and she has no idea where that music is coming from. That's pretty funny, but you'd be surprised how accurate this analogy is. Girls have A LOT going on up there - all the time! Schedules, health, money, relationships, work, clothes, kids, and feelings are just a sample of the "tabs" that are open at any given time. Often simultaneously. Most of the blame for this, I think, comes from girls' predisposition to be worriers. By nature, they just tend to be more anxious than guys. This isn't necessarily a bad thing, though. In fact, most girls will probably outlive us because of this tendency to overthink things. She, most likely, won't be the one getting pushed down a hill in a shopping cart while holding a sword in one hand and sparklers in the other pretending to be a magic knight-wizard. (Totally not speaking from experience). But she will be the one who has already dialed 911, has bandages in her purse, and knows how to stabilize you till the ambulance arrives. You see, girls worry a lot, but they also have this amazing ability to use that worry to their advantage by forming it into something useful. Instead of being crippled by it, worry becomes planning. It becomes organization. It becomes research. It becomes determination. Girls make worry work for them! Now just try to imagine how much computational power all this takes up. It's no wonder girls seem to have something on their minds at all times. Because they do! They have a very difficult time getting their brains to "shut off". Then, just to complicate matters, sometimes the worry they have IS just plain ol' worry. It becomes necessary, now and then, to take a time out and just stop for a while to let her mind settle. Just like a computer, to make it run smoother, sometimes you have to let it defrag. Give it time to reorganize the files and reboot. Girls need to do the exact same thing. They need to reorganize their thoughts, purge some unnecessary ones, and reboot. How do they do that? With peace and quiet. Unfortunately, most girls won't allow themselves to stop. There's too much to do. Too much to worry about. That's where you come in. You need to help her to stop. You need to create an environment where it's ok to do nothing, just for a little while. Take the kids away for a few hours. Turn the TV off. Do the dishes. Fold the socks. Clean up the mess she's been asking you to clean up for a week and a half. Get things done that need to be done so she won't have to worry about doing them. It's almost as though girls have to give themselves permission to stop and do nothing because their brain says there's always more to do. Fill out the permission slip for her. MAKE it ok for her to do nothing. Quiet time is healing for her.

Help her find it.

15

DANCE WITH HER

I am NOT a dancer. You'll never find me boot scootin' or cha-cha sliding at a wedding reception. I've never been clubbing or anything like that. Other than slow dancing – I'm out. Chalk it up to being self-conscious or embarrassed or whatever. I just don't do it. Now, my wife, on the other hand, has no problem getting out on the dance floor. She'll join in the line dances and go cut loose with her friends. She likes it. And I like that she likes it. She needs to have fun. And I'm perfectly content watching from the sidelines. That is until the D.J. says he's gonna' "slow things down," then I go and meet my girl on the dance floor. There's just something special about a slow dance. For her, it creates a unique emotional connection. The closeness and intimacy of it can be intoxicating. You touch. Your focus tightens. And if you do it right, it can feel like it's just you and her on that dance floor. It's like a snuggle that sways and spins and, even though you're in the middle of a hundred other people, makes her feel like she's the only girl in the room and that she's safe and secure in your arms. Oh, and don't worry if you're not a very good dancer; she's just happy that you're out there with her.

Don't let the fear of a few missteps cause you to miss these rare moments of connection. They really are something special. That being said, if you really want to turn up the special dial, try asking her to dance at other times; when it's unexpected. If she's had a long day, put on one of her favorite slow songs, offer her your hand while she's sitting on the couch, lead her to the middle of the living room, hold her close, and dance with her. It's amazing how much stress this will diffuse in her. She may even start crying. That's a good thing. Just keep dancing with her until SHE is ready to stop. Another idea is when you're sitting in the car, maybe watching the sunset or listening to the rain, turn the radio up, get out of the car, and dance with her right there in the driveway or parking lot or field or wherever. (Bonus points for dancing in the rain). Wherever you do it, show her that she's your only dance partner. Let her feel that she's safe in your arms. Show her that she always makes your heart dance and you don't want anyone cutting in.

JOSHUA WESOLEK

16

REMEMBER THE
SPECIAL DAYS

Quick! When's your anniversary? Did you forget? It's not today, is it? Yikes! Sorry guys, didn't mean to stress you out there. Well, not really. I do hope you knew the answer. If you did, awesome! Good for you. If you didn't, don't worry, I won't tell, but you need to figure it out when you get done reading this! Remembering the special days in your relationship is SO important when it comes to making your girl happy. I can't tell you how many times I've heard girls tell stories about how their guy forgot their anniversary or birthday or Valentine's Day, etc. It's devastating to them. "How could he forget?" Hmm, how COULD you forget? Oh, so many ways. First of all, let's face it – our brains are different. Your girl's brain contains a computer-generated spreadsheet of EVERYONE'S special dates! She knows the birthdays of everyone in her family, including aunts, uncles, nieces, nephews, cousins, even her cousin's babies! She has detailed lists of holidays, anniversaries, and every significant event that has taken place in your relationship. Now, unfortunately, when it comes to OUR brains, those lists of dates sorta' look like we wrote some notes on our hand about a week ago. Some, we can barely make out. Others are worn away completely. Another reason we forget is that guys tend to live in the now. We go through life one day at a time. Today, we're gonna' deal with today. Tomorrow, we'll deal with tomorrow, and things tend to sneak up on us. Whereas girls, on the other hand, tend to be planners. Girls may physically be here today, but mentally, they're three weeks in the future. Lastly – and I think this is the biggest reason – guys forget special dates because they're just not that big of a deal to him. Woah! WHAT? I know. That sounds bad, but don't get ahead of me. What I mean by that is guys typically aren't big on sentiment. We don't really need to commemorate special occasions in our life with gifts or celebration or get mushy over memories. Heck, our own birthday is just another day. For the most part, guys just don't need that stuff. However, just because WE might not need these affirmations – YOUR GIRL DOES! She loves to relive happy memories. Girls are way more emotional than guys and they place heavy significance on special dates and milestones in your relationship. When you started dating. When you shared your first kiss. The first time you went to a concert together, and so many more. All these moments are part of the beautiful, unique story of your relationship and forgetting them can make her feel like you don't find your relationship that important. Especially if you forget your anniversary. That's the day you two became a couple, or more importantly, husband and wife, and she might see your forgetting it as meaning that you don't think the beginning of your relationship was important enough to remember. And if the beginning wasn't important, then what about now? Celebrating these occasions is very important to your girl. That means it needs to be important to you, too. Guys, please, do whatever it takes to remember the special occasions. The birthdays. The anniversaries. The first times. Put them in your phone. Write them on a calendar. Heck, actually write them on your hand. I don't care! Just remember! This lets her know that you absolutely do value your relationship. It proves that your story is important, and it shows her that you understand that every occasion with her is a special one.

Made ya' look!

You're halfway through the book! Awesome!
YOU GOT THIS!
KEEP GOING!

JOSHUA WESOLEK

17

P.D.A.

Yes. That kind of P.D.A. Public Display of Affection. Usually, when we hear this term, there seems to be a negative vibe that goes along with it. I think the reason behind that is the fact that most people think of a P.D.A. as some gross couple blatantly making out and groping each other on a park bench or in the checkout line at the grocery store. That, "Get a room!" sort of P.D.A. I'm not talking about that. I'm talking about holding hands when you're out walking, or giving her a little kiss across the table when you're out to dinner. Let her sit on your lap when you're at the park. That sort of thing. Displaying your affection doesn't mean bringing what should be private out into public. It means just what it says – displaying affection. Maybe we're confused about the "affection" part. What exactly does that mean anyway? Affection is simply defined as a gentle feeling of fondness or liking. Gentle. Not gross. Just enough to let the public know that, "Hey, I like this girl and we're together." Simple, right? Well, unfortunately, lots of guys out there do NOT participate in ANY sort of P.D.A. No hand holding. No kissing. No hugging. In private? Yeah. Of course! He can't keep his hands off her, but in public, he almost treats her as a stranger. There could be several reasons for this, such as upbringing, religion, or a shy personality. Some guys consider it to be a sign of weakness and are afraid that one of their guy friends might see him holding hands. OH MY! They'd think he was such a wimp or that he's so "whipped." That's nonsense. The reality is, the public is mostly indifferent to simple P.D.A's. They could care less if you do or don't. But there is someone who does care – a lot. That's your girl. You not showing any affection out in public can make her feel like you are embarrassed of her. She might think that you don't want anyone to know you're a couple. Even if neither of those things are true, this is the perception you create. It makes her feel unimportant. Guys, let's be real. Your girl is the most important person that you'll encounter in public. Treat her like it. Not just at home. *Don't let WHERE you are change WHO you are.* Show her that you're proud to be her man. Show everybody! Holding her hand in public is kinda' like silent bragging. "Hey everyone, look how lucky I am!" Because, let's face it, we really are. She's the best thing in our lives, and when you let the world know, she'll know it too.

18

DON'T BUY HER
ROSES & CHOCOLATES

Wow. . how romantic. . roses and chocolates – again. . how thoughtful of you. (If you weren't sure, that line is dripping with sarcasm!) C'mon guys. Let's be real about this. Giving this as a gift EVERY Valentine's Day or anniversary is a cop-out. What? You look confused. Don't worry, I get it. Society and marketers have us trained to think that a dozen (or more) roses and a heart-shaped box of chocolates is the most romantic gift combo ever imagined. Well, they're WRONG. Even so, florists can barely keep up with the demand on Valentine's Day, and retailer's chocolate displays get wiped right out. Why? Well, because it's easy. It doesn't require any thought. You don't have to know what size t-shirt she wears or what movie she would love to own so she can watch it over and over or what her favorite body wash is. It's just grab and go. I'm sorry guys, but that's NOT romance. – that's cliché. Not to mention ridiculously overpriced! My wife has forbidden me from buying her roses on holidays because I could put that money toward something much better than some flowers that are gonna' die in 5 days. That dozen roses you just bought for $49.99 on Valentine's Day cost $14.99 two weeks before. They're scamming you. They're counting on you to take the easy route.

They're counting on you to forget and scramble at the last minute so you're willing to pay those exorbitant prices. Basically, they're counting on you to be a "typical guy". Don't be a stereotype. YOU'RE BETTER THAN THAT! You're with your girl because she sees something special in you. Show her that you see something special in her too. Give her a candle-lit massage. Write her a note – with an actual pen and paper. Make her dinner (it doesn't even have to be good, trust me). Just make it personal. Anyone can give roses and chocolates; but she's not just anyone, now is she?

DISCLAIMER: If you're in a new relationship, roses and chocolates are perfectly acceptable because you're just getting to know each other. But once you get to know her better – make it personal.

19

BUY HER
ROSES & CHOCOLATES

Huh? But didn't you just say. . .? Yes, yes I did. I also thought that using this heading next was pretty funny. Hey! It's my book! Moving on.   No, I'm not contradicting myself here. Roses and chocolates — together or separate — are perfectly fine to give as gifts. There's just one major catch. SPONTANEITY. Don't give her roses on Valentine's Day. Give her roses on . . . Wednesday! Leave some chocolates by her phone with a little love note before you go to work. That's great! Oh, and It doesn't HAVE to be roses and chocolates. You know what she likes. Instead of roses and chocolates, my wife prefers wildflowers and gummy peach rings. Mix it up. I work second shift, so when I get home, she's asleep. Sometimes, I'll stop on the way home and pick up a single rose, put it in a vase, and leave it on the counter for her with a note for when she wakes up for work. Not because it's her birthday or any sort of holiday. It's just because I love her and I know it will make her smile in the morning. And THAT'S THE SECRET, the randomness of it. The surprise. That's what makes it special. Never underestimate the power of flowers delivered to her work "for no reason" to brighten up her entire day, put an unstoppable smile on her face, and maybe even make all the other girls a little jealous! It's not really about the flowers or the candy, it's about making her smile. Letting her know that you're thinking about her. It's showing her that you don't have to wait for a special occasion, holiday or birthday to buy her flowers, because to you, every day with her is special.

JOSHUA WESOLEK

20

DON'T HANG UP WITHOUT SAYING, "I LOVE YOU"

What if the last time you talked to your girl was the LAST time you ever talked to her? What would she remember? Would your last words to her be, ". . .and don't forget to pick up some dog food, uh huh, bye?" Are those the last words she'll have to treasure if you were suddenly gone? I know, it's kind of morbid to think about and God forbid anything would happen to you, but in this uncertain world, you just never know. What I do know is, for me, I want her last memory of me to be a positive one that reinforces my love for her. The Bible reminds us to let our conversation be always full of grace. I try my best to hold to that with everyone, but I especially want that to hold true with my wife. I always want our conversations to be pleasant. No matter what we're talking about, no matter how brief the interaction, I always want it to end on a positive note. Am I perfect at it? Nope. But one small way I can try to ensure that happens is by ending EVERY phone call with, "I love you." It seems simple, but you'd be surprised at how many guys end phone calls with their girls with a passive, "uh huh, bye." It might seem silly, but words are powerful. Especially LAST words. You should treat every chance you get to talk to her as a gift. Even if it's just a quick call to ask her where your keys are – she's still there to ask – and you should be thankful for that every time she answers. That's why, no matter what, the next time you talk to her on the phone, tell her you love her before you hang up. If that should happen to be the last thing she ever hears you say, that's a gift that her heart will never forget.

JOSHUA WESOLEK

21

LEAVE NOTES

Our lives today are so inundated with emails, tweets, texts, and snaps that we almost don't even have to talk to each other anymore. Much less do we ever have to write anything! Remember that? Writing? With an actual pen and paper? If it's a little fuzzy, trust me, you're not alone. Writing something down is becoming more and more rare as we move to an increasingly digital and virtual world. It's not hard to see why, though. Writing takes EFFORT. Shooting a quick text or snapping a pic is almost second nature to us now. It's quick, easy, and we're done. But writing takes a little more time, a little more preparation, and a little more care. Written words don't automatically fall in straight lines in "Arial" font. There's no auto-correct or predictive text. IT'S ALL UP TO YOU. Your style. Your penmanship. Your little smiley faces. It's personal. And that's exactly what makes it so special. When's the last time you wrote your girl a letter? Middle School? What about just a little note to say, "I love you?" I'm telling you, there's something different about a handwritten note. It's hard to explain, but notes just "feel" better than a typed memo or a text. Before the days of cell phones, I wrote my wife (my girlfriend then) notes all the time. Every night before I left her house, I'd tuck her in, gather my things, grab the magnetic notepad off the fridge and write her some sort of note and leave it on the kitchen table for her to see the next morning. It was never anything long, just a quick note about something we'd talked about that day, or a simple "I miss you already," a little stick-figure drawing or even just the word, "someday." ("Someday" was a recurring theme of our talks referring to the someday that we would get married). Even though they were just simple notes, she TREASURED them. In fact, she still has all those notes in a shoebox in the attic. She told me that it made her smile when she saw the notes because she knew I thought about her one more time before I went out the door. I still leave notes today, although not nearly as much as before. (Darn texting!) It might be an "I love you" sticky note on the cupboard or a lipstick heart on the bathroom mirror. Whatever it is, I'm taking the time. I'm thinking about her. I'm leaving a part of me with her, not some digital text to be deleted. Take the time to write your girl notes. You'll be surprised how nice it is for you to slow down for a second, think about her, and write down that thought. IT DOESN'T HAVE TO BE A MASTERPIECE, just a little piece of what's in your heart. Trust me. She'll love it.

22

JUST SNUGGLE

WARNING!
SERIOUS SELF-CONTROL REQUIRED AHEAD

It's bedtime. It's been one of those days. She's a little stressed. You both go to bed together. She's looking cute in her sleep clothes – as usual. As you settle in under the blankets, she lets out a deep, relaxing sigh. She slides back into you to be the "little spoon" and puts your arm around her and holds it tight. Oh, boy! GAME ON! Right guys? Well, let's pump the brakes there, Turbo. I get it. It's nighttime, you're both in the bed and she's in close proximity. The perfect recipe to get handsy since she's *obviously* in the mood. STOP RIGHT THERE! Let's be honest. Guys are pretty much always in the mood. We aren't really that complicated. We automatically assume that spooning leads to. . .well, you know, other utensils. But girls aren't so simple. Most of the time spooning is just that – spooning. Just a snuggle. No agenda, no foreplay. It's a chance for her to feel safe, protected, and cared for so she can finally let her guard down and just let go of the day. She can finally relax. At this point, letting your hands wander or making suggestive comments can actually sabotage this time for her. Might even make her a little angry. Remember, she's trying to let go of the stress of the day and interrupting that can be very counter-productive. Let her rest. Let her unwind. Let her breathe. When she's done that, who knows, maybe she'll initiate something else – or maybe she'll fall asleep. EITHER WAY, you're being there for her the way she needs you to be. You're putting her needs before your own. You're helping her let it all go. If you really want to score some points, try initiating a cuddle session yourself. Don't go into it with an agenda. Just be there for her. Be selfless. Help her to stop everything, be quiet, and just rest. Sometimes she just needs to snuggle.

Be her favorite place to do just that.

JOSHUA WESOLEK

23

WRITE HER A POEM

Yeah, I know. I think I just actually heard your collective eyes roll. Just bear with me. I know this can be intimidating and you might even consider it emasculating, but trust me, there are some major points to be won here! Most girls LOVE poems. Even if they say they're corny or sappy – deep down, they love them. There are a bunch of reasons why. Poems are romantic. They're pretty. The rhythm and rhyme of them is like a spoken song written just for them. But at the heart of it, what they really love is the fact that you wrote it. You took the time (sometimes a LOT of time) to come up with a personal expression of your feelings for her. Every time she reads it, she'll think of you. Poems are powerful. They don't even have to be that good, either. They don't have to be some long, Shakespearean masterpiece. *Verily, thou dos't not need to encumb'r thyself by trying to speaketh in early English to maketh thine words soundeth better.* You just need to make sure it comes from your heart. For example:

> "Roses are red
> Violets are blue
> I'm not great at poems
> But I really love you!"

Short, sweet, and to the point. See guys, writing a poem doesn't have to be scary or complicated. Just put a little effort into it. Believe me, she'll appreciate it. If you're a "man's man" and she knows you had to take time out of rebuilding that engine or rounding up 100 head of cattle to tap into your sensitive side to write her one, she'll appreciate it that much more. It's not really about the poem, it's more about the effort. Whether it turns out goofy, or corny, or sappy, to her, it'll be perfect. Oh, and yes, you can use the poem up there, but after that, no more freebies. Take the time. Make the effort. She's gonna' love it. Verily!

24

BE CREATIVE

Let's talk about gift giving. Whether it's a birthday, anniversary, or holiday, you're going to be doing it. Often. I absolutely love giving gifts. You've heard the phrase, "It's better to give than to receive?" That's me all the way. In fact, I always feel awkward being on the receiving end. I never know how to react. What if I don't really like the gift? What if I do really like it, but I don't respond excitedly enough, etc.? Anyway, the point is, I like giving gifts way better. I love watching my girl's eyes light up. I love seeing her smile. The anticipation of her opening something I know she'll love is a rush. There's also a challenge to it, as gift giving evolves over time – or at least it should. The longer you're with someone, the more meaningful gifts should become. The better you know her, the better you should get at knowing what she likes and dislikes. When my wife and I started dating, teddy bears and cassette tapes were perfect gifts. But as time went by and the stuffed animals piled up, it was time to move on from the cliché gifts to something more creative. What's that? Oh, you're still scratching your head about the cassette tapes? They're little plastic rectangular devices that music used to be recorded on. After 8-tracks and before CD's. . . not helping? Sorry, you'll have to Google it. We need to get back on topic. Being creative with your gift giving takes work. You can't just run into the store, grab something pink and something sweet and call it good. You need to know what she likes. Sometimes even without her telling you. Getting her something she didn't even ask for but that you know she'll love is one of the best kinds of gifts. Now, let's take it a step further. Don't just be creative about WHAT you give her. Be creative about HOW. Make gift giving an experience. Remember, girls are emotional creatures. Oftentimes, they will remember how the experience of receiving a gift made them feel more than the actual gift itself. Of course, she'll remember what you got her (girls don't forget anything – I'm throwing that one in for free), but sometimes it's how she got it that makes the most impact. Don't be the "typical guy." Stand out. Do things differently. Put some effort into it. For example, instead of going out to her favorite restaurant and handing her a present, how about making a menu insert and taking your gifts to the restaurant ahead of time. When you get there,

let her order off the "special menu" and have
the server bring the gifts out to her. Maybe
you could arrange a scavenger hunt to several
meaningful locations around town and be
waiting with gifts at the end. Maybe you could
take her shopping somewhere full of small
mom and pop shops and have the clerks in
several stores give her gifts, seemingly at
random, that you'd pre-arranged. Wow. That
seems like a lot of work. Yeah, it can be. But
maintaining a strong relationship takes work;
and believe me, your efforts will be rewarded
when you see the huge smile and surprise on
her face. The examples above are, indeed,
involved, but you don't always have to go
extreme. Simple things can be just as
memorable, like having flowers waiting in the
hotel room when you go away for the
weekend. You could leave a note and her
favorite treat in her car for her to find when
she gets out of work. It's all about the
unexpected. Catching her by surprise. Don't
just give gifts. Give her an experience. It
makes an impact on her heart that will last
forever. Just like the impact she's made on
yours.

25

DON'T LET HER LOSE HERSELF

I'm gonna' aim this one at moms. Whether your girl is a working mom, or a stay-at-home mom; whether you have one kid or ten kids, I think this one applies to all moms. Moms are AMAZING! They can do anything and everything – and often do. They are a miraculous mixture of housekeeper, cook, nurse, accountant, teacher, therapist, personal shopper, secretary, and pretty much anything else you and the kids need her to be. Sometimes, on top of all that, they also have a "regular" job. I'm in awe of what my wife does in our household. I work in the foundry, and I tell her all the time that she works way more than I do. And therein lies the problem. Moms work twenty-four hours a day. There are no union-negotiated breaks in motherhood. The more demands the household makes, the more she steps up. The more needs her kids have – including her big kids (yes, I'm talking about you and me), the more she gives. My wife will wake up at 6:30 because she's "thinking about everything I have to do," have a load of laundry in the washer by 6:35, and be out to the grocery store by 7:00. Next thing you know, it's bedtime and she's exhausted because she's been "mom-ing" all day. Moms give their all to their families. They make innumerable sacrifices. One of the greatest ones I'm hoping to counter here, is the sacrifice of her identity. See, before your girl was "Mom," she had a name. She had a reputation. She had friends and hobbies. She went shopping at stores that didn't sell milk and diapers. She actually bought things for herself. But slowly, somewhere along the line, moms start to lose that identity. Well, no, they don't really lose it, rather, they willingly set it aside and start assuming the role of Mom. She chooses to live less for herself and more for her family. Over time, that identity she set aside gets packed away and harder to get to. And because this was a choice she made, you will seldom hear her complain about it. But you need to realize that there is still an individual in there. There's a girl that wants to go out with her friends sometimes. A girl who wants to laugh and be the girl she remembers from her more carefree days. A girl who wants to get away and be herself for a while. Am I saying she wants to give up all this mom stuff? Of course not. What I'm saying is, she NEEDS a break. And you may need to push the issue because her mom identity is strong. It's very difficult sometimes for her to unplug and step back for a second for fear that the household will spiral out of control. She won't think there's time to go out.   She won't want to go shopping for herself because the kids need things. You may actually find yourself debating with her to do something for herself! BUT DO IT. She needs it. If you have to dial her friend's number and put the phone in her hand, do it. Assure her that it's ok to go out. It's ok to have fun with her friends and spend some money and try on clothes and laugh and be silly. . . like she used to. It's ok. Even necessary. Yes, she's an amazing mom.   But she's also an amazing individual who needs some "me" time. Help her unpack the identity she boxed up – then make sure she always keeps it within reach.

26

STRAIGHTEN OUT YOUR SOCKS

Laundry.

The archenemy of women everywhere.
Seriously, whoever comes up with the first robot that will sort, wash, dry, fold, and put away the laundry will be the richest person who ever lived, this side of King Solomon. And also be elected President of the World.

Most women HATE doing laundry. Well, maybe hate is too strong a word. . . nope. They hate it! Especially moms. The dirty clothes are never-ending. In my house, my wife can empty the hamper, load the clothes into the washer, walk back to the hamper and find more clothes! It's seriously never-ending. I just wanna' make sure we're clear, laundry is the enemy. Ok. Now that we agree on that, let's move on. Years ago, I had a habit of taking my socks off inside out. You know, I sort of peeled them down from the top and they either ended up completely inside-out or in sort of a half-and-half clump. That's how I threw them in the hamper. So? Big deal, right? Well, no. Not really. It's just socks in a hamper. But over time, it became a big deal, and if I wouldn't have acted, it could've become a VERY big deal. What? It's just socks! Yes, but there's more to it than that. Little things can build up, whether good or bad. The snowball effect. And this one almost triggered an avalanche. So, there I was throwing my socks in the hamper all willy-nilly and thinking nothing of it until one day, my wife, in a sort of faux-irritated voice, said, "Ugh! Straighten out your socks!" Yeah, ok. Ha-ha. And that was it – or so I thought. Well, as time went by, I started to hear it more and more in less and less sarcastic tones. Then she started throwing them at me to "fix them!" I still wasn't getting the hint. But then, one day, she confided in a friend at church about my sock issue. Just seemingly normal "girl talk," but the fact that this issue had now expanded beyond her and I and she felt the need to tell someone else about it meant that this was really bothering her. In fact, the person she was talking with sarcastically threatened me if I didn't start straightening out my socks. I FINALLY got the hint and I've been doing it right ever since. Avalanche averted. Now, was this really all about the socks? Well, yes and no. Yes, the socks were the trigger, but it was more like the straw that broke the camel's back. Girls can get overwhelmed. They do SO MUCH around the house and beyond, I can barely fathom how it all gets done. It's pretty amazing. But she does get stressed. And, sad to say, a lot of that stress comes from a lack of help. (I'm looking at us guys.) If she's constantly having to do unnecessary tasks like cleaning up other people's messes, throwing away their trash, putting their dishes in the sink, or, yes, straightening out their socks before she can wash and/or fold them, yeah, she's gonna' get bitter about it. Especially when she asks for a little help and nothing changes. (See above. Face-palm at myself.) It's not really about the socks. It's one more thing she has to do. It's one more thing she SHOULDN'T HAVE TO DO. It's one thing you could've helped her with. Don't let something simple cause strife in your relationship. Watch and listen for ways to help her out. Throw it away. Rinse it off. Put it back where you got it from. She's got enough to do. Save her from having to take any extra, unnecessary steps like straightening out your socks! And if you really want to be her hero fighting against her archenemy, fold them and put them away too!

27

GO OUT OF YOUR WAY

Sorry guys, but being good to your girl isn't always convenient. Sometimes, making her happy takes some pretty significant time and effort on your part. For example, when my wife was pregnant with our first child, she woke up at 3 a.m. and wanted a Slurpee. Like, REALLY wanted a Slurpee. At 3 a.m. Also, we lived nowhere near a 7-Eleven. So, I had a choice to make. Do I whine because I'm tired and tell her to just crush up a popsicle or something, or do I suck it up, go get her a Slurpee, and make her happy? Well, obviously, I went, or why would I be telling you this story? But you know what, it made her happy and she still remembers that to this day. Why? *Because sacrifice makes an impact* – even relatively small sacrifices like a thirty-minute Slurpee run at three in the morning. Yes, she loved the Slurpee, but she loved the fact that I went to get it for her even more. Be careful, though. Nothing cancels out the appreciation of your efforts like doing something begrudgingly. Don't EVER make her feel like she somehow caused you to be inconvenienced. Especially since, most of the time, girls don't really expect you to go to ridiculous lengths to do nice things for them. But you should WANT TO. You shouldn't go into these types of situations selfishly with a, "she better appreciate this" attitude. You might as well not even do it. Instead, go into it happily focusing on the outcome - she's gonna' be so happy! When you see her smiling and surprised and maybe even speechless, the two-hour drive to pick up concert tickets is suddenly so worth it. The twelve hours of online searches and phone calls to find someone to fix a treasured possession of hers that broke that she thought she'd never get repaired – worth it. The extra hours you put in at work so you could afford a special gift for her that you know she'll love but would never expect – worth it. Remember, girls are emotional. Sure, she'll love the outcome of your efforts, but what she'll really remember is that you love her enough to make her happy no matter what. Now isn't that worth going out of your way for?

28

HUG HER WHEN IT'S HARD

Uh oh. She's mad at you. You two were arguing, emotions got high, words were exchanged, and now she's in the other room. Angry. Maybe even crying. She's at that "whatever" stage. Here's an idea, why don't you just jump right in there and give her a great big hug? What? What do you mean, "no?" You don't think she's in the hugging mood right now? And, what's that? You were right in that argument, so she should be apologizing to and hugging YOU? Alright, like I said, emotions are high right now. Let's step back, take a deep breath, and look at what's really going on here. I hate arguing (often referred to in a relationship as "fighting"). DISAGREEMENTS are ok. Even helpful sometimes. But ARGUMENTS are just too heated. Too emotional. Too angry. It's amazing how intense things can get between two people who love each other so much! But it happens – more than we like. But I'm not getting into the argument part. I want to focus more on the aftermath. The part when you're both in separate rooms nursing your pride and stewing over what just happened. Chances are, as a guy, you're re-watching the play-by-play in your head to make sure that what you said proved your point; thinking what you should've said that would've worked better, and "what was she even talking about!?" You might think she's doing the same thing, too. Scoring the fight to determine who won. Well, here's the thing - she's probably not doing that, and neither of you won. I've said it a lot, but girls are emotional. They FEEL the argument. We, on the other hand, are very analytical. We dissect and grade the argument to determine if the outcome was in our favor. But look, even if you were right, there is no winner here. Nothing in your relationship should ever come down to you versus her. You know what she's probably doing in there? She's probably wondering if you still like her. She's probably afraid that the relationship is suddenly dissolving. And I'm not just talking about the girl you've only been with for six months. I'm talking about your wife of fifteen years. It may not be rational, but emotions rarely are. There are times when my wife is upset about something and without realizing it, she takes it out on me. She'll snap at me, or be short with me, and sometimes, it becomes an argument. An ugly one too, because I didn't do anything. But regardless, we end up in separate rooms.

And this, guys, is when we have a decision to make. Do we just let the anger stay? Do we want to prove our point so badly that we're willing to separate ourselves from this girl we love until she admits she was wrong? And what if she was right? Do we just pout and give her the silent treatment for hours – even days? Or instead (and this can be SO hard), do we swallow our pride EVEN IF WE WERE RIGHT and realize that most arguments aren't worth creating a rift between you. Understand that the majority of the argument was probably produced by flared up emotions. Put yourself in her shoes. Remember that you love that girl more than anything. Then, right or wrong, go to where she is, apologize – you can do it – and hug her like you mean it. Don't get hung up on the apology part. It's really just saying you're sorry about the fight itself, not necessarily the content. You can deal with that when the emotions subside. But for now, just hold her. Reassure her that you love her even when you disagree. Show her that you're in this relationship for keeps. Let her see that you're on the same side. She might think that the damage is beyond repair, but it's amazing how much a hug can fix.

29

PRAY TOGETHER

DON'T SKIP THIS ONE!

I know, I know, religion? Really? Don't worry. It's just one entry and I promise I won't preach. This isn't a religious book, but I AM a Chaplain, so you had to know I'd sneak a little God stuff in here somewhere. It'll be ok. Keep reading.

Praying. Chances are, you're familiar with it. Even if the only prayer you know is saying "Grace" before dinner, that's fine, we can work with that. Simply put, praying just means speaking to God. There's a lot loaded into that simple definition, but for the purpose of this book (and to keep my promise of not preaching) that will suffice. So, why pray together? Why pray at all? Again, that's a sermon waiting to happen, but for now, let me skip to one extreme end of why. Chances are that sooner or later, whether it's you and your girlfriend, your fiancée, or your wife, you are going to wind up in a difficult situation that you won't be able to fix. It might be a financial crisis. It may be a dire medical prognosis. You might lose your job, your car, or your home. You may even lose a loved one. In any case, we, as guys, are going to do everything we can to try and salvage the wreckage, fix the problem, and move on. That's what we do.

We're fixers – until we're not. There's going to come a time when all options have been exhausted. All avenues have been explored. Every rock you know of has been turned over, and you will be at your wit's end. You might yell, cry, throw things, and plead. It will feel like no one in the world has an answer to your problem and that you're all alone with nowhere to turn. THAT is a perfect time to pray. Just tell God what you're going through and ask for His help. Yeah, it's that simple. You might be surprised at the relief you feel because you're finally transferring the responsibility of fixing this seemingly impossible issue that you've weighed yourself down with over to God. Now, it's in His hands, and, if you let Him, He'll show you the way forward because nothing is impossible for Him. But, why pray together? Because you're a team. Because there's strength in numbers. Because you don't need to fight alone. Bring her in to your struggle. Be honest with her. She was created to help and support you. LET HER. When the two of you pray together, there's unity. When the two of you pray together, it strengthens your relationship because you're facing the challenges side by side. You're both leaning on each other, and together, leaning on God. Then, when the answer comes, you can celebrate together knowing that, with God's help, you stayed by each other's side through incredible hardship and what God puts together, no one can take apart. Of course, during a tragedy isn't the only time you should pray together. Pray when things are good. Pray when she's sad. Pray when you're anxious. The more you do it, the easier it gets, and the closer you'll become to God AND each other. "But what if I don't believe in any of this God stuff?" Well, again, to spare you the sermon, I'll simply say, "try it." Just be sure to bring her along when you do. That way you can both share in what happens next.

If you have any questions about praying or any other God stuff, look up and visit a local church together. They'd love to help.

30

BE HER SAFE PLACE

You did it! You made to the end of the book. Good for you. Just the fact that you read through this whole thing shows that you're serious about being the best boyfriend/fiancé/husband you can be. After all, your girl deserves your best, or, what's the point? Every day, she's bombarded with the pressures of society. She's shown how she should look, act, talk, and dress. She's following social media that paints an impossible picture of the "perfect" girl and "relationship goals." But everything she sees is a dramatization. That's not real life, but whether she realizes that or not, there is still an unspoken standard that she holds herself to. That's why she needs you. She needs to know that when she's with you, she can just be herself and know that you accept her as she is – flaws and all. She needs to be able to TRUST you enough to be vulnerable and show you the scars from her past knowing that healing is possible and her secrets are safe. She wants to feel that you support her and her decisions, and when she's with you, that she can finally let her guard down. She can laugh, cry, dream, and rest. You need to be her safe place. I truly believe that if you take the advice written in this book to heart, you will be on a well-lit path to becoming that place for her. Am I saying that this book is fool-proof? Not at all. But I AM saying that through the years, my relationship has grown stronger and stronger by following the principles in it. I'm also not saying your journey won't be without trials, and some of the topics in this book can be hard to put into practice, but you're on the right track. You made it through the book! Heck, just the fact that you read it in the first place proves that you want what's best for her, and that you're willing to work for it. You've already made it past the hardest part – looking for help. So, I encourage you to keep it up. Keep on going, even if you mess up. Be the best guy you can be so she can be the best she can be. You can do it. She needs you. Be there for her how she needs you to be.

Be her safe place.

You got this.

JOSHUA WESOLEK

Want some more tips on how to treat your girl better? Here's a description from the Bible of what love is AND isn't:

Love is PATIENT and KIND
Love DOES NOT envy or boast
It is not arrogant or rude
It does not insist on its OWN WAY
It is not irritable or resentful
It does not rejoice at wrongdoing,
But REJOICES with the TRUTH
Love BEARS all things
BELIEVES all things
HOPES all things
ENDURES all things

Love never fails

1 Corinthians 13:4-8

Thank You.

Made in the USA
Monee, IL
09 January 2020